Italy

A Guide to the Must-See Cities in Italy!

By Sam Spector

Table of Contents

Introduction

Hi, my name is Sam and I first of all want to thank and congratulate you for purchasing my book, 'Italy: A Guide to the Must-See Cities in Italy!'

Italy is an amazing country filled with fascinating historical locations and a deep, vibrant culture. Each of the cities in Italy offers something different to its visitors: from the fairytale canals of Venice to the Ancient streets of Rome. All are unique in their own way, and have different sights and attractions to explore and enjoy.

The Italian people are exciting and animated, always willing to stop for a chat. As you visit each new city you will find that the locals take to you with a warm smile and an open heart, and will often be eager to help you when you look lost.

What I hope to achieve in this book is to provide you with a reliable guide on exactly what to see in each of Italy's major cities, and how to navigate your way around the country to see as much as humanly possible.

I will give you the top ten of my personal favorite things to see and do in each of the top ten cities in Italy, as well as a description of exactly why you simply can't miss them. I will provide insights that I've gained from my own extensive travel throughout Italy, and some tips for making the most out of your own Italian trip.

I wish you the best of luck with your future travels and want to thank you again for purchasing my book. Never stop traveling and never leave any stone unturned.

Chapter 1: Milan

The fashion capital of the World, Milan, should be the first stop on your Italian adventure. Why? It provides the perfect starting point for your journey, being at the very top of Italy, and also provides the cheapest flight destination in the whole of Italy! Of course this is no excuse to simply fly in and continue on your merry way, without first exploring everything that this sophisticated, magnificent metropolis has to offer.

Aside from being a fashionista's dream city, Milan is also a leading economic powerhouse, being the main industrial, commercial and financial center of Italy. It hosts Italy's main stock exchange, and is home to the majority of major banks and corporations in Italy. Don't let this bore you, however!

As a major world fashion and design capital, there is an array of museums, theaters and unique landmarks to stoke your inner flame of creativity. Allow the city's unrivaled shopping opportunities, booming nightlife and prestigious air of elegance sweep you off your feet into a land of sheer enjoyment.

The Top Ten

A sight which emanates the creativity and passion of the city it is in should be first on your list to see in Milan. Such a sight can be found in Duomo, Milan's wondrous, pink marble cathedral. Set in an extravagant Gothic theme, the cathedral is without doubt one of Milan's most remarkable attractions to behold, and the view from atop the structure is unparalleled. The vast interior of the cathedral is just as impressive, with some of the largest and most inspiring stained glass windows to be found in the World.

On the outskirts of the magnificent Duomo sits the esteemed Museo del Novecento. This rather modern art museum provides works from 20th century artists such as Boccioni and Campigli, and provides a welcome distraction for the eyes as you walk about its collection. Its chronological rooms will inspire you as you walk through them, whilst also providing an insight into the Italy's transition through Fascism, the two World Wars and its projection into an age of technology.

One of the city's greatest treasures, and one that is talked about in elitist circles and popular culture alike throughout the World, resides in a humble refectory in central Milan. Possibly the World's most famous mural, The Last Supper by Leonardo Da Vinci, sits within the Convent of Santa Marie delle Grazie. To see this ethereal beauty you must book well in advance, or join in any city tour which will undoubtedly pass by the masterpiece.

Indulgence is a term which comes to mind when thinking about the culinary delights Italy has to offer. One place where you can explore the full meaning of this term is Peck, Milan's historic and famous local deli. Here you can enjoy an almost endless selection of Parmesan cheese, pastries, seafood, cold meats, caviar, truffle, olive oils, vinegars, pralines, chocolates and freshly made gelato!

There is no better place to discover why Italy has such a firm culinary reputation than this quaint yet comprehensive deli.

With your understanding of Italian culinary delicacies intact, it's now time to partake in some fine Italian wine tasting. Milan, being capital of the most famous wine district of Lombardy, provides the perfect place to develop your wine palette. Whether you're a complete novice or wine connoisseur, a wine tasting class is sure to delight anyone looking to enjoy the delicious product of local grapes.

Being in the fashion capital of the World, you would be amiss if you did not at least peruse the wares of this shopper's Mecca. It's little wonder than Milan's upscale fashion shopping district is known as the Rectangle of Gold. With its constant display of designs by the elite Armani, Dolce & Gabbana and Prada, you will feel as if you are strutting the cat-walk as you walk along its streets. The merchandise in most of the shops you'll visit will definitely be out of your price range, but the window shopping here provides enough enjoyment without the need to break the bank.

When Milan's esteemed fashionistas elect to clean out their closet of designer labels, they often find their way into vintage shops, such as Cavilli e Nastri. This vintage emporium is regularly swept over by locals looking for the next bargain of hidden fashion treasure, but if you're lucky you may be able to find a pristine piece of art from the fashion archives to proudly display on the streets of Milan.

To really kick a goal on your exploration of Milan, there is no better place than San Siro Stadium! Milan's premium sporting venue is home to two Italy's most famous football clubs: AC Milan and FC Internazionale. If you get the chance to watch either team play here, the atmosphere created by the echoing shouts and cheers of passionate fans is an amazing experience. If you don't get the chance, at least visit on a non-match day to tour the museum and stadium, including a peak into the dressing rooms of both teams.

When it comes time to have dinner you could opt for one of Milan's most refined and classy restaurants, all of which boast a wide array of fine food and wine. While they do provide a great experience, you should at least one of the nights of your visit choose a more mobile dining option. The ATMosfera is a vintage tram service which tours the city at night, providing a spectacular way to see the sights of the city, and they serve up a fine dinner with wine while you travel!

To close out any night in Milan, you have countless options to enjoy the sparkling nightlife the city possesses. One of the prime sources of entertainment is the Navigli District surrounding the city's historic canals, which boasts many bars, restaurants and entertainment venues. Mag Cafĕ is a firm starting point for your evening adventures, which provides cocktails which have been expertly concocted to have you in high spirits in the shortest amount of time possible. Only good things can happen after a visit to this fine establishment.

Chapter 2: Turin

The city of Turin possesses a rich culture and history, stemming from its once eminent position of Italy's first capital city. Although it is not as politically significant as it once was, the city is now a major European crossroad for industry and trade. The architecture of Turin has crossed many phases of history, and still holds displays   of renaissance, baroque, rococo, neo-classical,   and art nouveau architecture.

Turin provides a subtly enjoyable experience as you explore its many boulevards, nouveau cafes and stunning buildings. Due to its positioning, Turin is often referred to as the 'capital of the Alps', being only a short trip to the beautiful peaks of the mountain range. The city is also a center for innovation, giving the World its first taste of hard chocolate as well as giving birth to the popular Fiat car.

The Top Ten

The symbol of Turin can be seen from every corner of the city and its image is spread far and wide throughout Italy, due to its inclusion on the Italian two-cent coin. Mole Antonelliana is a 167m tall tower within the heart of the city which was originally intended to be used as a synagogue. The tower also provides the most stunning view over Turin, and as you ascend the Panoramic Lift you might find yourself getting dizzy as gaze out from the unobstructed viewing platform!

Another landmark of near equal importance is the Duomo di San Giovanni. The cathedral of Turin, taking its place since the late 15th century, is quite beautiful to gaze upon but the real intrigue of this attraction is within its intrinsic myth. The church is home to the famous Shroud of Turin, the claimed cloth within which the body of Jesus was wrapped upon his burial. A duplicate cloth is on constant display beside the altar within the cathedral, and many Christian and non-Christians alike flock here to view the piece.

There exist several esteemed palaces which are strung throughout central Turin, but the most appealing of these is certainly the Palazzo Madama. With the beginnings of a fortified castle, it includes influences of both Medieval and Baroque periods within its striking facade, and the interior is just as eye-catching. Each of the four floors found within the palace now represents somewhat of a museum, with the inclusion of stonework, paintings, porcelain, embroideries, and Roman and Renaissance artwork.

A sight which overshadows one of Turin's other famous palaces, the Royal Palace, is the Royal Church of San Lorenzo. Although the pastel facade is subtly brilliant to view, the interior of this Baroque gem is what really sets it apart. Its incredibly high altar is one of the most elaborate in all of Italy, and the features which surround it more than support its magnificence. With wooden carving, colored marble, oil paintings and a physical layout which encourages the light to dance forth from the high windows all around, it is an experience that won't soon be forgotten.

A favorite treat for both locals and tourists, and one which is sure to win over any hot chocolate or coffee lover, can be found at Al Bicerin. First established beneath a 14th century bell tower, this cafe provides the renowned bicerin, a hot caffeine drink consisting of a delicious concoction of hot chocolate, coffee and cream. Allow this warm, rich liquid to excite your taste buds and replenish your energy, so you're more than ready to continue your adventuring.

Feeling revitalized and re-energized, your next stop should be to the iconic Museo Nazionale dell'Automobile. Being the home of one of the world's leading car manufacturers, Fiat, its fitting that this title is celebrated by this fantastic motor car museum. Not only Fiats are on display here, with Peugots to Ferraris also making a dashing appearance. This museum will take you on a journey exploring car culture, technical qualities and societal problems such as pollution and congestion, so it is an interesting experience for car lovers of any level.

While there the daylight still lingers in the sky, be sure to visit Parco Valentino. This enormous, 550,000 square meter park is consumed by joggers, walkers, sun-bathers and lovers at any time of the day or night. Walk through its grounds and long the River Po which runs beside it, and its beauty will help you understand exactly why it is so frequently visited.

As evening begins to set over Turin and your stomach begins to grow louder, what better way to subdue your hunger than with some traditional Italian pizza? If you ask any local where to go for the best pizza in Turin, the response will be the same: Sfashion pizzeria. With an entertaining and bold interior and hot, rustic pizzas flying out of the oven to feed the hungry mouths of the masses, this is one restaurant you don't want to miss.

To unearth a rather different experience of Turin, partake in the Turin Underground Evening Tour. Not too far beneath the bustling city of Turin lies a series of mysterious tunnels linking to certain cellars of Baroque palaces strewn through the city. The tour includes sites of ancient unsolved murder mysteries as well as an anti-raid war shelter along its long passages.

To delve into an even more mystifying part of Turin's history, you must explore the city's link to the dark occult. The Black and White Evening Magic Tour provides a look of Turin through a different scope, focusing on a half of the city which portrays good 'white magic' and one which emanates evil 'black magic'. Sinister architecture, frightening stone gargoyles and ancient spiritual buildings are all part of the experience.

Chapter 3: Genoa

This amazing Mediterranean jewel has been crowned 'The Proud One', and as you enjoy the majesty of Genoa, you'll find that it does indeed have a lot to be proud of. In the past it has also held the title of European Capital of Culture, thanks to its rich gastronomy, music, art scene, unique architecture and interesting history. In past times the city was a shipping and steel working center, and today its financial importance lives on, being home to many leading Italian companies.

The vibe as you walk through this town is more similar to a Caribbean port town than a French economic powerhouse, and for all the right reasons. The city itself is a charming maze of narrow, winding lanes where you will find old men smoking cigarettes outside of roaring bars, and prostitutes patrol the streets, but this doesn't detract anything from the city, but instead adds to its intrinsic charm. Ultimately Genoa will provide sights and scenes unlike any of the more reputable cities to be found in Italy.

The Top Ten

The largest physical display of Genoa's ancient history can be seen in one of the city's main attractions; the Walls of Genoa. Large portions of the wall still remain, and today Genoa has longer walls than any other Italian city. There are sections from various times throughout history, but the most prominent landmark along the stretch is the looming, intact gate of Porta Soprana.

The literal and spiritual heart of Genoa, and what is the next attraction you should explore, is the Medieval Old City. Famous for its narrow, criss-crossing lanes, a walk through the Old City is an adventure which could last you an entire day - as long as you don't get lost! Bars, shops and cafes line the streets during the day, but it's at night when the Old City really comes to life.

The largest claim to fame in Genoan history is undoubtedly that of the birthplace of explorer Christopher Columbus. Many residences throughout the city insist they were the childhood home of this legendary navigator, but the one with the most merit is certainly Casa della Famiglia Colombo. This attraction provides an interesting insight into his history, upbringing and rise to greatness.

Much has changed in Genoa over the years, but one thing that remains omnipotent and ever-present is the lone sentinel of this great port, La Lanterna. Commanding a dominant position from which to guide all ships into port in the darkness of night, this iconic lighthouse is one of the oldest and tallest, and still works to this day. Visitors can traverse a pleasant 800m walk to the lighthouse, climb its 172 steps and learn its role in the history of Genoa.

Several palaces and mansions make for interesting viewing in the city also, but the one you should visit above all others is Palazzo Reale. With exquisite gardens, fine furnishings, an extensive collection of artwork and an entire hallway of impressive mirrors, you'll leave with a wanting for it to be your own private mansion!

One of the most relevant sights in Genoa, one which pays homage to its place in medieval and Renaissance maritime history, is the Galata Museo del Mare. This 'museum of the sea' presents technological exhibits tracing Genoa's history as Europe's once greatest port, the journey through sail and steamboats, and several interesting film exhibits. The top floor also presents one of the best views out over the city, the perfect place for taking memorable photos.

To partake in an authentic culinary taste experience, Trattoria del Raibetta provides all this and more. This snug little restaurant provides regional dishes inspired by fresh seafood, and possesses an endless list of vintage wines to enjoy.

Porto Antico, the port which once controlled an empire, now has a more modern twist and presents itself as one of the best attractions to explore. It presents the perfect place for an evening stroll after a satisfying dinner, and there are even a few attractions for children to enjoy. Il Galeone Neptune is one of such exciting exhibits, being a full-size replica pirate ship that is now an enjoyable playground for all ages.

Another attraction appealing to all age groups and every demographic is the city's large Acquario. This amazing aquarium is one of the largest in Europe, with thousands of fish, sharks and other aquatic creatures swimming amongst six million liters of water!

Although Genoa's shoreline is picturesque, to paint a picture you won't forget in an entire lifetime, take a day trip to the awe-inspiring Cinque Terre. This string of villages presents one of the most colorful of untouched, Mediterranean beauty to be found anywhere in the world. Miles of spectacular rocky coast, remote fishing villages, vineyards cultivated into stone walls, promontories and pristine aquamarine waters are a few of the things you can look forward to on this breathtaking trip!

Chapter 4: Verona

Verona is a city out of a story tale, literally. With three famous Shakespearean plays being set in the city of Verona, it has earned a wide tourist following and is highly regarded as a place of significant artistic heritage. Romance, drama and intrigue have been present within Verona for centuries, dating back to its humble origins as a Roman trade center in 3rd century BC.

In more recent times Verona became one of the leading promoters of Fascism, being a key transit point for Italian Jews to be sent to Nazi concentration camps. Today the city represents one of Northern Italy's most international, commercial centers and is World Heritage listed by UNESCO due to its astounding urban structure and architecture.

The Top Ten

One of the first attractions to view in the Verona was one of the very first built over the span of the city's long history. The Roman Amphitheater, a vast structure of pink marble dating back to the 1st century, became the city's famous open-air opera house seating around 30,000 people. It is still used as such today, especially throughout the summer opera festival.

A look back into a somewhat more recent past is provided by the Museo di Castelvecchio. This former fortress was severely damaged by Napoleon in battle, and later by the WWII bombings, to the point where it was almost beyond repair. Instead of destroying it or completely restoring it, however, it was reinvented. Bridges have been made over exposed foundations, massive holes filled with glass and every piece of damage being accentuated in this way, not hidden. It allows a sense of being thrown back into the time when such ravages occurred to the impressive structure.

Another piece of Roman heritage is present within the Piazza delle Erbe. With the origins of a Roman forum, the plaza is now a buzzing, meeting point of cafes, buildings and shops. Nearby to the Piazza sits the Arco della Costa, which possesses an unusual trademark. A whale's rib is hung above the arch, and legend says that it will fall upon the first just person to walk beneath it. Just people must be hard to come by, because it is still intact today!

Within this bustling city plaza sits an attraction in its own right, Caffè Filippini. Providing a vast contrast between itself and the surrounding calm of the city, this late-night 'cafe' specializes in the creation of their own Filippini, a frothing cocktail of vermouth, gin, lemon and ice that is sure to put a kick in your step.

To the nearby south-west of the Piazza delle Erbe resides Verona's historic Jewish Ghetto. It was here that the heroine Rita Rosani commanded a band of followers in Verona to oppose the treatment of Jews during this time, sadly being caught and executed at the age of 24. The Jewish Synagogue in the area is always open to visitors who want to learn more about the areas history.

On hot days it can be hard to walk between every sight of Verona and not find yourself drained, despite how wonderful they are. Remedy yourself against overheating with a quick stop to Gelateria Ponte Pietra. This esteemed gelateria makes all of its delectable gelato on sight, and possesses many favorites including (but not limited to) candied orange, white chocolate and hazelnut, and the special mille fiori, with one of its key ingredients being pollen gathered from the nearby local hills of Verona.

A recurring theme which is apparent among the magnificent cities of Italy is the presence of equally magnificent cathedrals. Verona is no exception. The Duomo found here is an grand, striped structure is impressive without being overly extravagant, mostly due to its perfectly balanced interior, and the inclusion of several exceptionally crafted statues.

For fans of Shakespeare's works, and in particular of Romeo and Juliet (which I presume is all of us), Casa di Giullietta is a sight no loving soul can miss. The famous balcony of the fictional star-crossed lovers of Romeo and Juliet is frequented by lovers every day, to recite their own vows of love, and to live out their very own fairytale romance.

To dine in style is not necessarily everyone's kind of dining, but to dine with exquisite food and sumptuous tastes should be on everyone's list of desires. The Pizzeria Du de Cope can fulfill this desire, with crispy, delicious pizzas being provided at affordable rates. Watch your pizza rise to greatness in the oven over the counter top before consuming it in the dashingly colorful dining space.

Crossing the river Fiume Adige which runs through Verona, you can stumble upon the wonderfully refreshing Giardino Giusti. Considered a masterpiece of Renaissance landscaping, these gardens present various forms of vegetation sculpted to perfection. Walk its grounds and be amazed by the fine detail to which Mother Nature is tamed by the talented sculptors of the garden.

Chapter 5: Venice

To a city which is on the bucket list of travelers worldwide, and one that more than lives up to its reputation, Venice. Situated on a group of 117 tiny individual islands and connected only by small, elaborate bridges, canals act as the highways of this magical 'City of Water'. Venice is world-renowned for its beauty, both natural and architectural, and its unique layout has gained the city, along with its lagoon, World Heritage status.

Widely regarded as the most beautiful city in the entire world, the 'Floating City' of Venice deserves every accolade it receives. It has become a wealthy city throughout history, thanks to its significance as a trade center and maritime power throughout the Middle Ages and Renaissance period, along with its innovation of several artistic and musical movements.

Venetian feasts are to be had, songs to be sung and masquerades to be enjoyed. The grandeur of this epic city will forever remain in your heart and mind upon leaving the city, but while you are here enjoy it to the fullest - it's an experience you won't soon forget.

The Top Ten

To begin your majestic Venetian experience there is no better way than to travel the lengths of the famous canals themselves. I recommend to walk first among the charming squares, over quaint bridges and through narrow alleys, before taking a guided tour with a means of transport unique to the city: by gondola. The iconic gondolas of Venice provide the perfect means for exploring the Grand Canal and smaller canals, as you learn of the city's colorful past, view distinct attractions and gain access to some lesser known sights. A gondola ride provides a romantic experience for couples and an equally enjoyable experience for individuals.

One of the more grandiose sights to be viewed in Venice (which is saying something) is the Basilica di San Marco. The signature church of Venice boasts domineering spires, lustrous mosaics and extravagant marble structures, but the treasures hidden within represent its true beauty. Gold is found everywhere within the church, lavishly decorating much of the interior, with the center piece being the Pala d'Oro, the magnificent golden altar. The museum and treasury inside the structure also give an interesting recount of much of the city's history and glory.

Another attraction with a magnificence befitting of the city within which it resides is the Palazzo Ducale. This grand, Gothic palace dates back to the 9th century and holds a firm place in the glorious history of Venice. Once being a lavish residence, it is now merely aesthetic indulgence for any tourist who walks its halls. The second floor chambers provide the highlight of this lavish mansion, with epic paintings strewn across the walls and the magnificent throne of Venice's chief magistrate, the Doge.

Venice doesn't attempt to hide its title as one of the culinary chiefs of Italy, possessing countless fine dining establishments. But for tourists with a more modest budget, Taverna del Campiello Remer provides an excellent alternative. Bargain-hunters will love this secluded restaurant perched on the Grand Canal, with generous buffet-style meals and delicious pasta dishes for just €20. Possessing a command of the Italian language is not necessary but will help at this venue, as the sign states: menú turistico non ghe xe (no tourist menu to be found here)!

Yet another piece of stunning Venetian architecture and craftsmanship is the Scuola Grande di San Rocco. Many artists commissioned to paint this marvelous building, but the artist that won out did so by creating a wonderful ceiling panel for the structure. The painted scenes to be found inside tell a story of Venice's glory, historic importance and magnificence.

With regular Venetian buildings possessing such beautiful artwork, its difficult to imagine the beauty of the works that can be found within Venice's Gallerie dell'Accademia. Words fail to describe the contents of this historic gallery which include works from 14th to 18th century geniuses including Tintoretto, Canaletto and Bellini. The loose layout of the gallery makes for an enjoyable experience as you stumble upon masterpieces one after the other, cherishing every second you spend here.

Supplying many of the esteemed five-star restaurants of Venice is a market which holds fresh, seasonal and local food above all other codes; Rialto Market. Soft-shell crab, baby octopus and squid are a few of the regional Venetian specialties which can be sampled in the market. Not limited to seafood, the produce to be found here is also second-to-none, with inclusions of ripe tomatoes, bright red peppers and sweet, seasonal strawberries which are sure to delight any food lover.

One of the esteemed restaurants which gets its seafood fresh from the Rialto each and every morning, and one with a taste for all things fresh, is Osteria alla Staffa. This restaurant puts a twist on some Venetian classics in a delightfully playful way, and is frequently packed with hungry mouths to feed. If you can't find a seat when you visit, try some scrumptious dishes at the bar instead.

To toast the sun as it sets in the Venetian sky, look no further than Al Prosecco. This popular wine bar utilizes organic ingredients to create intriguing taste sensations within its wines and cocktails. Try the wild yeast fermented wines here for a real treat and a the perfect start to an amazing night out in Venice.

Although you may be hard-pressed to find a reason to leave the wonderful city, a few hours' drive of Venice lay the majestic Dolomite Mountains, which do their best to beckon you out of the city - at least for one day. A day trip to these mountains will not end in regret, with the landscape and lakes surrounding them being some of the most picturesque you will ever witness.

Chapter 6: Bologna

A city with origins dating back past many other famous Italian metropolises, Bologna was first settled around 3,000 years ago! The city has played a part in shaping much of the known World, once being the fifth most populous city in Europe, and surviving throughout its lengths of serving various ruling populations. It is home to the oldest University in the entire World and to this day is a bustling, youthful center of social and cultural wonder.

The city is one of the wealthiest in Italy, and is constantly ranked among the top cities in terms of quality of living. The architecture to be found here includes works from many of the various ages it has seen, and paints a picture of the city's history. The city today is somewhat of an amusing contradiction, being both a rich, high-tech and important trade center and a political, radical and edgy student hub. The mix is delightful to behold, and enables you to encounter many interesting people within any given day in this fantastic city.

The Top Ten

The oldest university in the World is certainly a claim to hold bragging rights over, and one which makes the University of Bologna a must-see attraction. The red brick buildings which make up the university blend in with the surrounding cityscape, but the architecture of many of the main halls are of a grander scale than the buildings around it. The university also possesses several museums to visit, some of which are free.

If there were to be an overarching symbol of Bologna, Le Due Torri would hold this title. Bologna's two leaning towers stand watch over the Piazza di Porta Ravegnana and peer down upon onlookers from high above. One tower does so more than its counterpart, with the taller of the two towers, the 97.6 meter tall Torre degli Asinelli perched much higher than the smaller Torre Garisenda, which is blocked off due to its dubious 3.2 meter tilt. The taller tower can be scaled by the brave, although local student legend says that if you climb to its peak you will never graduate!

The most audacious of Bologna's tourist attractions is the Basilica di San Petronio. This mammoth church, the fifth-largest in the World, is a Gothic Giant plunked in the heart of Bologna. Its main facade was never finished during construction and today still remains incomplete, but this gives the basilica an interesting appearance of uncertainty. The huge 68 meter-long sundial within the church is the crowning sight and has a vital place in history, discovering anomalies leading to what was the creation of the leap year.

Italy is the only country in which you can really justify dessert *before* your meal, and La Sorbetteria Castiglione fully justifies this conviction. Although it sits towards the outskirts of the main city, this gelato haven is well worth the trip, with its sweet, frozen balls of heaven sure to make your taste buds dance.

The logical sequence is of course to follow Italian gelato with an Italian meal, and where better than Drogheria della Rosa? This former pharmacy still showcases glass jars and wooden shelves, but now is known as a rather high class trattoria, inclusive of mouth-watering Bolognese specials such as juicy steaks and sumptuous pastas.

After such a moving taste one-two combination, you may find yourself inspired to learn to recreate such a culinary experience with your own hands. To learn to achieve such expertise in the kitchen, Bologna offers several esteemed cooking schools to help you achieve this feat. One of the most renowned and reasonably priced is La Vecchia Scuola Bolognese, which will have you making cloud-soft gnocchi in no time!

Of the numerous extravagant palaces, mansions and castles in the region, one stands out above all the others: Palazzo dell'Archiginnasio. It today contains the 700,000 books of the Biblioteca Comunale, as well as the 17th century Teatro Anatomico, where bodily dissections were once held, overseen by an Inquisition priest.

For a detailed, guided walk down Bologna's nearly 3 millennia-long memory lane, simply visit the Museo della Storia di Bologna. As you progress through the 34 chronologically ordered rooms of this epic museum, you'll discover many interesting and otherwise hidden facts about Bologna, as well as an explanation of how it became the city it is today.

As the night comes drawing nearer and your anticipation to experience the buzzing nightlife of this chic city, one of the key inclusions on your night out has to be Le Stanze. This former chapel has each of its four main rooms converted to possess their own unique theme, within which you can enjoy a wine or cocktail accompanied by some delicious paella, pasta or even juicy chicken drumsticks!

A stop which never disappoints and one which is a favorite of many locals is Bologna's number one jazz institution, Cantina Bentivoglio. This part snooty wine bar, part smoky jazz club gives a cozy feel to its patrons as they engulf one (or several) of around 500 wines on offer and soak in the smooth jazz vibes! With nightly performances you may find yourself returning to this venue upon multiple nights to relive its electric atmosphere.

Chapter 7: Florence

The city of Florence is a Mecca for vagabonds and highbrow tourists from the all over the world, being one of the most frequently visited destinations in Italy. It is famous for its comprehensive history, being one of the wealthiest cities of all time, considered the birthplace of the Renaissance and even being named the "Athens of the Middle Ages".

Along with such historic titles it has also been crowned as one of the most beautiful cities in the World, being a showcase of Renaissance architecture and possessing several striking monuments. The many galleries of the city allow tourists a look into the beginnings of the Renaissance movement, and the influence of the time period upon the World today. Spend a few days in Florence and you'll find yourself utterly absorbed by its beauty and prestige; spend longer and you'll find it hard to leave!

The Top Ten

Florence may be the home city of Renaissance artwork and culture, but Galleria degli Uffizi is the physical home of the greatest collection of Italian Renaissance art to be found anywhere in the World. This prestigious gallery includes works by the likes of Botticelli and Leonardo da Vinci, and provides entertainment for hours as you look upon the many masterpieces of the Renaissance period which fill its halls.

The Duomo of Florence is one which holds a place as one of the city's most iconic landmarks. Its facade consisting of pink, white and green marble commands attention from afar, and its regal bell tower dominates the skyline. A steep, rather claustrophobic climb of 463 steps will allow you to gaze down at a view over the city almost as beautiful as the cathedral itself.

A palace which has a rather modest facade for once, but one that still exudes greatness, is Palazzo Vecchio. From outside it stands strong and unflinching, a fortress palace originally erected for the city government. Inside allows a little more indulgence, with painted hallways and the statue of the Genius of Victory by Michelangelo present. From atop the palace's roof you are able to take in an astonishing view to top it off.

Whether it's breakfast, lunch or dinner, Il Teatro del Sale is a restaurant which provides both ample food to satisfy your hunger and ample entertainment to tickle your funny bone. The Florentine chef here is a wonderful mix of ingenuity and eccentricity, and if you come for dinner you will witness firsthand thanks to performances put on by he and his comic wife. You must pay a very small annual membership to dine here, but this gains you access to an exclusive and very entertaining club which you'll be glad to be a part of.

Undoubtedly you'll be wanting to buy some souvenirs to remind your friends or family back home that you went on the trip of a lifetime and they didn't, and there is nowhere better to find the perfect souvenir than on Ponte Vecchio. This Medieval stone bridge has shops inbuilt along it, which are occupied by a range of art dealers, jewelers and souvenir sellers. Try not to look like too much of a tourist to get the best deals!

To one attraction which draws crowd day in and day out, at all times of the year. The Galleria dell'Accademia, and specifically the magnificent Statue of David by Michelangelo which is contained within, is truly worth whatever wait you must endure to view it. The statue has the most strikingly subtle details to be found on any sculpture, and can seem to change as you gaze upon it from various angles. There are other works in this gallery, but it is this masterpiece which deservedly gains the majority of admiration.

Forte di Belvedere was designed not to be an extravagant and lavish living residence, but as a means of foreign protection. Even so, the fort is impressive as you walk about its grounds and learn of the many soldiers which were once housed here to protect against the threat of foreign invasion.

If electing to participate in one of the many fine dining experiences Florence has on offer, do yourself a favor and elect to try Il Santo Bevitore. Reserve a table if you don't want to risk going without a seat, and then relax as you are seated in this classy, tasteful and creative gastronomic marvel. The dishes to be tried here are many and diverse, as Florentine classics are deconstructed and recreated in exciting new flavor combinations.

For an intimate and quite special experience, Le Volpi e l'Uva is a must. This charming wine bar boasts an impressive list of Italian wines and is the perfect place to take a lifelong partner, or a new friend you have recently met on the streets of Florence. The Tuscan cheese on offer here complements the selection of wines quite nicely too.

To escape the city for a day or two, there is much to see and do around the beautiful area of Tuscany. Walking the grounds of Chianti Vineyards is a serene experience and the Gothic city of Siena is famous for its medieval streets, but there is one stopover you cannot miss on your travels: a trip to the city of Pisa. If you are a sucker for classic, touristic photo opportunities, they don't come much greater than this. Prop your leg or hands up in the air against the Leaning Tower of Pisa for the perfect gravity-defying photograph!

Chapter 8: Perugia

Perugia is known as the 'Universities Town', because although it doesn't possess establishments which predate that of the University of Bologna, they sheer quantity of tertiary institutions within the city trumps that of any other Italian metropolis. As a result, Perugia is widely regarded as a cultural and artistic center of Italy, possessing several famous painters and architects throughout its history.

The city is propped upon a hill overlooking peaceful fields, and consists of a mix of winding cobblestone alleys, various impressive mansions and several grand archways connecting its many streets. The students of Perugia ensure the city exudes a culture of sheer enjoyment, with boisterous partying and pleasure to be found around every corner.

The Top Ten

The Palazzo dei Priori is one of the finest establishments to be found in Perugia, and one of the first that should be on your list to visit! This Gothic palace can be seen from afar and stands out from the bland buildings around it with its ornate, yet subtle facade.

Within the Palazzo is housed another gem, the Galleria Nazionale dell'Umbria. This institution is the finest art gallery in Perugia, and indeed in the entire larger area of Umbria. It holds within its halls a remarkable 3000 works of genius from the 13th century until the Renaissance period, and includes famous pieces by several local artistic heroes.

With golden ticket in hand, you can visit the magically delicious world of the Perugian chocolate factory, or Casa del Cioccolato Perugina. A tour includes both a visit to the sweetly informative museum and an exploration of the factory itself, where the magic really happens. If you're lucky you might uncover the secret recipe for the dark, brown gold of Perugia!

In true solemn Perugian style stands the city's somber, giant cathedral, Cattedrale di San Lorenzo. Not nearly as lavish as some of the cathedrals to be found in Italy's other major cities, this cathedral provides a sobering normality which allows you to focus more upon the striking Gothic architecture to be found both inside and out.

If an adopted Italian family is just what you've always dreamed of, La Taverna can certainly make this dream come true. This humbly named restaurant has staff that will treat you like on of their own (kids), as they take you in off the street and prepare a homemade pasta dish sure to satisfy even the largest of appetites. Just don't try to refuse a second serving!

Somehow you'll have to find room in your belly for a sweet treat as you stumble upon the wonderful Sandri. Serving coffee and cake to locals since the middle of the 19th century, this Perugian favorite also provides a delectable assortment of cakes, pastries and chocolates.

You may at some point in your trip decide to forgo the endless supply of amazing restaurants and prepare your own meal (at least once). If doing so, to give yourself the best possible chance of recreating something resembling that of an Italian feast, shop at Umbria Terraviva! This organic market provides a wide range of fresh fruits and vegetables to work with.

Predating the city's Roman ancestry is Perugia's history as a key center of the Etruscans. Although now a long time ago, the remnants of this ancient past can be viewed at the Arco Etrusco. These Etruscan gates aren't necessarily of an epic size, but its impressive to imagine they were constructed nearly 2 millennia ago.

As sun sets and the colors of the Perugian sky begin to blend together into darkness, it's time for the city to come alive. Begin your night's adventure at the La Terrazza, an open-air venue where you can sip away at drinks while still contemplating what to make of your evening ahead.

With enough liquid courage built up you will now be ready to hit the Perugian party scene with full force! Velvet Fashioncafĕ is where the rich, poor, bland and beautiful all come to mingle in an elegant display of dance and entertainment, and to party into the late hours of the night. There is no better way to conclude an intriguing day in this great city than to lose yourself here in music and pleasure.

Chapter 9: Rome

A city with an ever-endearing people, a beautiful, rich culture and a heroic past which has left a greater mark on the World than any city in history. Rome is truly one of the most amazing cities ever to have existed throughout any time period, including the present day. The site of the city has been occupied for thousands of years, making it one of the longest continuously occupied cities in Europe. The actual city of Rome has seen over two and a half thousand years of history, which includes the rise and fall of one of the greatest military and political powers in history; the Roman Kingdom.

Regarded as one of the key birthplaces of Western civilization, Rome has been at the forefront of many significant movements. It has been the main instigator of each of the Renaissance and Baroque periods, with its influence upon architecture, art and culture being eminent throughout Italy. Rome is also the only city in the World to contain a separate country within its confines, being the famous Vatican City.

The landmarks of this standout city are some of the most distinct and recognizable to be found anywhere, bringing countless tourists into the city each year. The allure of Rome is not due to attractions alone, however. The vibe which is omnipotent and forever present throughout its streets, buildings and people are more than enough to make you consider running away to Rome and never, ever coming back - if only for a second.

The Top Ten

There is no point in wasting time in a city with so many amazing things to see, do and experience! So to start your unforgettable Rome experience, visit the most colossal of the city's sights; the Colosseum. The greatest of gladiatorial combat was once undertaken here, with blood, triumph and death all occurring to the endless cheers of the Roman people. Today the sight is nothing short of remarkable. The pure sight of the exterior will send shivers down your spine, and the interior is just as inspiring.

From a temple that worships blood to a temple of a more spiritual worship, this next attraction is just as divine. The Pantheon has played an equal, if not greater, part in the history of Rome. It has stood the test of time for some 2000 years, and is one of the best preserved ancient monuments in Italy. Originally built by Hadrian to worship the classic Greek Gods of old, it is regarded as the Ancient Roman's greatest architectural achievement.

The Piazza di Spagna is an area of Rome with possibly the highest concentration of tourists throughout the entire city! From the magnificent Spanish Steps you can get a bird's eye view of the people below, which provides for great people-watching of the tourist and local variety. With spying aside, the view from the steps of the surrounding city and sunken fountain below is very pleasant.

If you plan to see each of the unique and inspiring art galleries within Rome, you may need to extend your trip! There are indeed a great magnitude of fantastic art museums to visit, but one you simply cannot miss is Museo e Galleria Borghese. This esteemed museum holds what is considered to be the greatest of all private art collections, boastings works by Botticelli, Raphael and Bernini. It is an experience no art connoisseur can afford to miss.

If the pasta is good in Italy, it is fantastic in Rome and is pure heaven at Da Danilo. This popular restaurant is vaunted as having the best carbonara in Rome, and rightly so in my opinion. Cooked to perfection, with the most subtle flavors added their dishes in just the right proportions, it is a taste experience that will leave you begging for more.

Continuing on your whirlwind landmark tour, next on your list of must-sees is the glistening Trevi Fountain. This epic Baroque fountain is the largest and most well-known in Rome, possessing a range of mythical creatures, majestic horses and rock formations over which the aquamarine liquid flows. There exists a famous tradition implemented for luck, which is to toss a coin into its waters over the left shoulder using your right hand. This is clearly a popular custom, with over €3000 thrown into the fountain daily!

For both religious crusaders and ordinary individuals, the next sight should prove to be equally exciting. The Sistine Chapel is the single place within the Vatican which every traveler wants to visit, and for good reason. It contains two world-famous works of art by the artistic genius Michelangelo. The remainder of the Chapel is equally impressive from both inside and out, and a tour of the confines provides and intriguing insight into the history of Roman Catholicism, as well as the process behind the election of the beloved Pope.

To find a delightful treat, one which is a necessary Italian indulgence, seek out the quaint Bar Pompi. This small patisserie provides a vast range of delicious Italian sweets, the most delectable of which are its variety of tiramisu. From classic coffee or cocoa, to pistachio or even Nutella, there is something to cater for every sweet-tooth!

There are outstanding cathedrals, and then there is St Peter's Basilica. In a league entirely of its own, this beloved Roman church is undoubtedly Italy's most spectacular. Its interior include several masterpieces of art, one by the brilliant Michelangelo, and a cavernous main hall to walk through. If you can make the trip to the summit of the church's signature dome, you will be in for a real treat as you find yourself with a breathtaking view over Rome.

With attractions done and dusted, it's time to relax and enjoy the city and its wonderful people. The perfect setting for such an occasion is Circolo degli Artisti, where you can mingle with local types or meat like-minded travelers, all while you party to one of their constantly changing themed events. Come here for a start to an eventful evening, or stay until the early hours for one of the best nights out in Rome.

Chapter 10: Naples

This Mediterranean jewel has been a vital part of life for each of the empires that have called it home over the many Millennia. Naples played a vital part in the merging of Greek culture into Roman society, and has had a large influence on culture in Italy in general. Its port is one of the most significant in Europe, possessing the highest passenger flow in the continent and being vital for Italy's international trade.

Naples was the most heavily bombed city in all of Italy during WWII, and so much of the city has had to undergo vast transformations during the 21st century. This doesn't take away from its charm, however, as their comforting Mediterranean lifestyle still remains within their culture today.

There exist countless historically significant sites within close proximity to Naples, which is not surprising with its 27 centuries of existence. The city is synonymous with being the epitome of easygoing Mediterranean living, with crystal blue waters and never-ending sun, as well as being known as the birthplace of Italy's most prized possession: pizza! Their culinary expertise doesn't stop at pizza, though, with some of the best seafood, pasta and coffee in the World Naples will leave you craving more.

The Top Ten

The very first thing you must do when arriving into Naples is allow yourself to walk about the city and port in the early day sunlight, to appreciate the city in full glory. As you wander through the streets you can gaze around at the overwhelmingly colorful buildings, smile at friendly locals who pass by and be amazed at the deep, clear water of the Napolese coastline.

Upon your journey around the city, be sure to stumble up Naples' oldest and greatest street market, La Pignasecca. This immaculate market provides an array of amazing produce and taste sensations including live seafood, creamy cheese and hearty wines. Its many delis are some of the best to be found in Italy, and some of its smaller street side stalls provide an interesting assortment of knick knacks and "designer" brand clothing, bags and perfume to catch hapless tourists unaware.

To peruse a collection of artwork which illustrates why Naples has held such a strong influence over Italian creativity, visit Museo Archeologico Nazionale. This premium museum is rapt with Greco-Roman culture, possessing one of the largest collections of such artifacts and works in the modern world. You can view numerous works of pottery, glassware, copper ware and learn about the discovery and maintenance of some of the key historic sites in the area.

Cappella Sansevero provides a place of both worship and intrigue for Napolese locals and travelers alike. This baroque chapel possesses one of the most incredible sculptures and one of the most famous of Italian works, Giuseppe's Veiled Christ. This sculpture alone is reason enough to visit the church, but the stunning architecture and many other striking statues provide ample justification.

Being in the heart of a city which is responsible for one of the greatest inventions on Earth (pizza) creates very high expectations. Pizzeria Gino Sorbillo lives up to these expectations and then some! This legendary pizza connoisseur is besieged each and every day by hordes of pizza-crazed and hungry individuals. The crowded and electric atmosphere in this pizzeria only adds to the experience, and the actual taste sensation is one you're not likely to find in any pizza ever again; so enjoy it while it lasts!

For the brave of heart and those who don't spook too easily, the Catacomba de San Gennaro provides a macabre yet interesting experience. This underground cemetery is typical of the Romans, and presents a gallery of the deceased through the remarkable design and artwork displayed on their tombs.

The mighty Complesso Monumentale di Santa Chiara is a spectacle of massive proportions. Being severely damaged during WWII, most of the structure had to be recreated to its original 14th century glory. Today it possesses an array of lavish tiles and frescoes to gaze upon, and a few beautiful remaining pieces from the original church.

A magical and thrilling entertainment experience is provided by Italy's largest and oldest opera house, Teatro San Carlo. The season runs almost year round, giving you ample opportunity to catch one of the many fantastic showcases on display here. If theatrics isn't your cup of tea, you can elect to take a guided tour of the grand opera house instead.

The wealth of historical landmarks and beautiful landscapes within close proximity to Naples is astounding. There are so many fantastic places to go in a day trip from Naples, the prime of which being the ancient site of Pompeii. The story of this lost city is something out of a fairytale, with the entire city and its inhabitants being destroyed during the eruption of a mighty volcano. Explore the ruins of this ancient city at your own pace and try to imagine the magnitude of destruction required to decimate such a city.

Traveling further east you will find one of the most beautiful sights of Southern Italy; the Amalfi Coast. If you have access to a car, or know someone who does, this coastline provides the most picturesque driving experience you will have in your entire lifetime. With a myriad of picture perfect places and towns to stop along the trip, you may find it difficult to keep driving - and to keep your eyes on the road!

Conclusion

Italy is a truly unique cultural experience full of wonder and beauty. Unfortunately for most people, seeing the whole of Italy's beautiful landscape from top to bottom isn't a realistic option.

What I hope to have achieved with this book is to have provided you with a guide how to get the most out of Italy in the limited time you may have. I would encourage you to stay here for as long as possible and soak up everything the country has to offer; the food, the culture, the people and every unforgettable experience. But if you can't, just make sure that you don't miss any of the cities I've mentioned and try to get to each of the attractions I've mentioned.

If you can make this round trip of Italy and get to all of the sights mentioned, I can guarantee you that you will have had the experience of a lifetime, and will have captured a significant glimpse of Italy's undeniably picturesque cities, landscape, architecture, ancient history and enduring culture.

I have no doubt that you will return at some stage in the future, hungry to see more of the beautiful, diverse and unforgettable country that is Italy.

Finally, if you enjoyed this book, please take the time to share your thoughts and post a review on Amazon. I would really appreciate it if you did.

Thank you and happy travels!

Made in the USA
Monee, IL
25 April 2022

95420533R00030